Autumn Leaves Shawl in Chenille by Barbara Herbster **2**

Collapse-Weave Scarf in Wool and Silk by Yvonne Stahl **4**

Blooming Leaf Chenille Scarf by Jean Korus **6**

Child's Play: A Winter Scarf by Liz Gipson **8**

The Mobi-Q Shawl by Margo Carr **10**

A Winter Scarf in Dornik Twill by Scott Norris **12**

Doubleweave for a Wool Ruana by Betsy Blumenthal **14**

Soft and Silky Warp-Faced Scarf by Suzanne DeAtley **16**

Silk Huck Lace Shawls for Spring by Ruth Morrison **18**

Spring Flowers Shawl by Helen Bobisud **20**

A Twill Scarf That's Light as Air by Marcella Laughlin and Mary Frost **22**

Night Windows Scarf by Barbara Weissman **24**

Lavender Shadows Scarves by Gudrun Polak **26**

Peacock Shawl in Shiny Tencel by Horace Lethbridge **28**

A New Millennium Quechquemitl by Sara Lamb **30**

Weaving and Finishing Scarves and Shawls **32**

YARN CHART

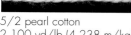
10/2 Tencel
4,200 yd/lb (8,470 m/kg)
20, 24, 28

5/2 pearl cotton
2,100 yd/lb (4,238 m/kg)
12, 16, 18

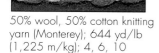
cotton novelty (Snowflake)
1,500 yd/lb (2,850 m/kg)
10, 14, 18

50% wool, 50% cotton knitting
yarn (Monterey); 644 yd/lb
(1,225 m/kg); 4, 6, 10

overtwisted 2-ply wool
12,600 yd/lb (7,460 m/kg)
30, 45, 60

2-ply (Shetland) wool
1,800 yd/lb (4,036 m/kg)
12, 15, 20

2-ply (Highland) wool
900 yd/lb, 1,700 m/kg
4, 6, 8

3-ply wool fingering yarn (Na-
ture-Spun), 2,800 yd/lb
(5,330 m/kg); 14, 18, 24

14/2 wool/alpaca
3,920 yd/lb (7,460 m/kg)
16, 20, 24

18/2 wool/silk
5,040 yd/lb (10,170 m/kg)
20, 24, 30

30/2 silk
7,500 yd/lb (15,840 m/kg)
24, 32, 40

20/2 silk
5,000 yd/lb (10,100 m/kg)
22, 26, 30

8/2 reeled silk
2,800 yd/lb (5,650 m/kg)
18, 20, 22

rayon chenille
1,300 yd/lb (2,620 m/kg)
12, 15, 18

rayon chenille
1,450 yd/lb (2,926 m/kg)
12, 15, 18

textured rayon chenille
(Chinchilla), 700 yd/lb
(1,330 m/kg); 8, 10, 12

100% viscose (Marbella),
2,325 yds/lb (4,425 m/kg)
12, 16, 18

75% rayon/25% cotton bouclé
(Pazzaz); 950 yd/lb
(1,800 m/kg);12, 16, 18

rayon ribbon (Glacé)
680 yd/lb (1,300 m/kg)
8, 10, 12

polyamide ribbon (Fettuchina)
1,150 yd/lb (2,190 m/kg)
8, 10, 12

AUTUMN LEAVES SHAWL IN CHENILLE

BARBARA HERBSTER

PROJECT AT-A-GLANCE

Weave structure

Plain weave with supplementary warp patterning.

Equipment

4-shaft loom, 20" weaving width; 15-dent reed; 1 shuttle.

Yarns

Ground warp: Rayon chenille (1,300 yd/lb), Black #002, 202 yd (2½ oz); Kensington #966, 208 yd (2⅗ oz); Purple Passion #098, 182 yd (2¼ oz); Wine #051 and Black Cherry #524, 108 yd (1⅓ oz) each; Paprika #113, Turquoise #138, and Citrone #240, 52 yd (⅔ oz) each; Tapestry Pandora #842, 13 yd (⅙ oz).

Supplementary warp: Fettuchina ribbon yarn (100% Tactile Polyamide, 1,150 yd/lb), Grape #540, 52 yd (¾ oz); Cassis #358, 33 yd (½ oz); China Red #565 and Licorice #002, 26 yd (⅜ oz) each.

Weft: Rayon chenille, Kensington #966, 750 yd (9¼ oz).

Yarn sources

All yarns are from Silk City Fibers.

Warp order and length

300 ends chenille, 42 ends ribbon yarn, 3¼ yd long (includes 30" for take-up and loom waste). Allow 2½ yd plus fringe for each additional shawl.

Warp and weft spacing

Ground warp: 15 epi (1/dent in a 15-dent reed). Supplementary warp: 15 epi (30 total epi in pattern areas). Width in the reed: 20". Weft: 13 ppi.

Take-up and shrinkage

10% in width and 10% in length. Amounts produce one shawl 18" × 82½" plus fringe.

I n my fabrics, the emphasis is always on color. I try to achieve a balanced look, but not necessarily a symmetrical one. I like to give viewers a little surprise in return for their attention.

Project notes

In this shawl, a plain-weave chenille ground cloth is patterned with supplementary-warp stripes of Fettuchina ribbon. The chenille ground cloth is slightly warp dominant to produce a soft drape and emphasize the many warp colors (only one color is used in the weft—this is a one-shuttle weave). Wherever three reds are used in the chenille warp (Kensington, Wine, and Black Cherry), their order is somewhat random. (Warping from back to front allows a bit of freedom to vary the color order as you select the warp ends to thread.) For simpler warping, you can reduce the number of colors in the chenille warp.

Beam the ground warp and the supplementary warp together and thread following Figure 1. Sley the ground warp 1/dent. Sley each supplementary warp end with its adjacent chenille ground end as in Figure 1.

Begin and end the shawl in plain weave with scrap yarn allowing 8" at each end for fringe. Weave 90" with Kensington chenille, following Figure 1.

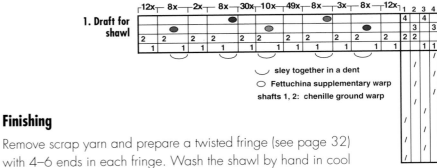

1. Draft for shawl

⌣ sley together in a dent
○ Fettuchina supplementary warp
shafts 1, 2: chenille ground warp

Finishing

Remove scrap yarn and prepare a twisted fringe (see page 32) with 4–6 ends in each fringe. Wash the shawl by hand in cool water, add fabric softener to the first rinse, and finish rinsing. Roll the fabric up, place in the washing machine, and spin out water. Machine dry on a cool setting.

2. Warp color order for shawl

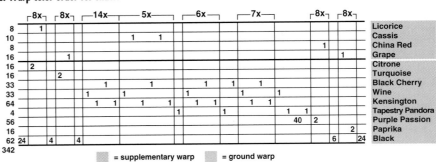

= supplementary warp   = ground warp

COLLAPSE-WEAVE SCARF IN WOOL AND SILK

YVONNE STAHL

PROJECT AT-A-GLANCE

Weave structure
Turned twill.

Equipment
8-shaft loom, 24" weaving width;
12-dent reed; 1 shuttle.

Yarns
Warp: 18/2 wool/silk (5,040 yd/lb),
Black, 864 yd (2¾ oz); Suede,
Sable, Basil, Curry, Copper,
Cinnabar, and Ruby, 120 yd
(⅝ oz) each.
Weft: 50/2 overtwist wool (12,600
yd/lb), black, 1,068 yd (1⅜ oz).

Yarn sources
Jaggerspun wool/silk (Zephyr) is
available from most retailers. 50/2
overtwist wool yarn is available from
The Handweavers Studio.

Warp order and length
568 ends 3 yd long (allows 38" for
fringe, take-up, and loom waste) following the warp color order in Figure
2. Allow 88" for each additional scarf.

Warp and weft spacing
Warp: 24 epi (2/dent in a 12-dent
reed). Width in the reed: 23⅔".
Weft: 22 ppi.

Take-up and shrinkage
66% in width and 9% in length.
Amounts produce one scarf 8" × 64"
plus fringe.

A class with Ann Richards on collapse weaves spurred me to experiment with collapse techniques. A turned-twill threading, an overtwisted weft, and careful finishing all combine to produce beautiful, lively collapse fabrics—particularly appropriate for scarves. If you are a spinner, you can enjoy experimenting with spinning your own overtwisted wefts for controlled effects. Fortunately for the weaver who is not a spinner, these yarns can also be found commercially.

Project notes

The draft in Figure 1 produces narrow alternate stripes of 3/1 and 1/3 twill. Even without an overtwisted weft, you'll notice as you weave that the 3/1 twill tends to puff upward and the 1/3 twill tends to puff downward. If the collapse is sufficient, one side of the cloth shows only the puffed-upward warp colors of the 3/1 twill and the other side only the puffed-downward warp colors of the 1/3 twill. For this scarf, Block A is black and Block B is a repeating sequence of seven different colors.The weaving is very quick and easy with one shuttle.

Allow 7" at each end for fringe. Begin and end with a small amount of scrap yarn. Weave the border, alternating blocks as indicated in Figure 1, weave 55–56" for the body of the scarf, and then weave the second border.

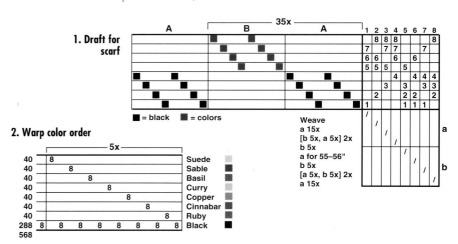

Finishing

Remove the fabric from the loom. Remove scrap yarn as you twist the fringe (see page 32) using the eight threads from each stripe as one fringe. Run very warm water into the kitchen sink and add one capful of Eucalan Woolwash. Place the scarf in the water and allow it to soak for ten minutes. Rinse, and then twist the scarf to remove excess water. Hang to dry (suspend from the fringe at one end) out of direct sunlight. The scarf will have collapsed to one third its weaving width and formed permanent pleats.

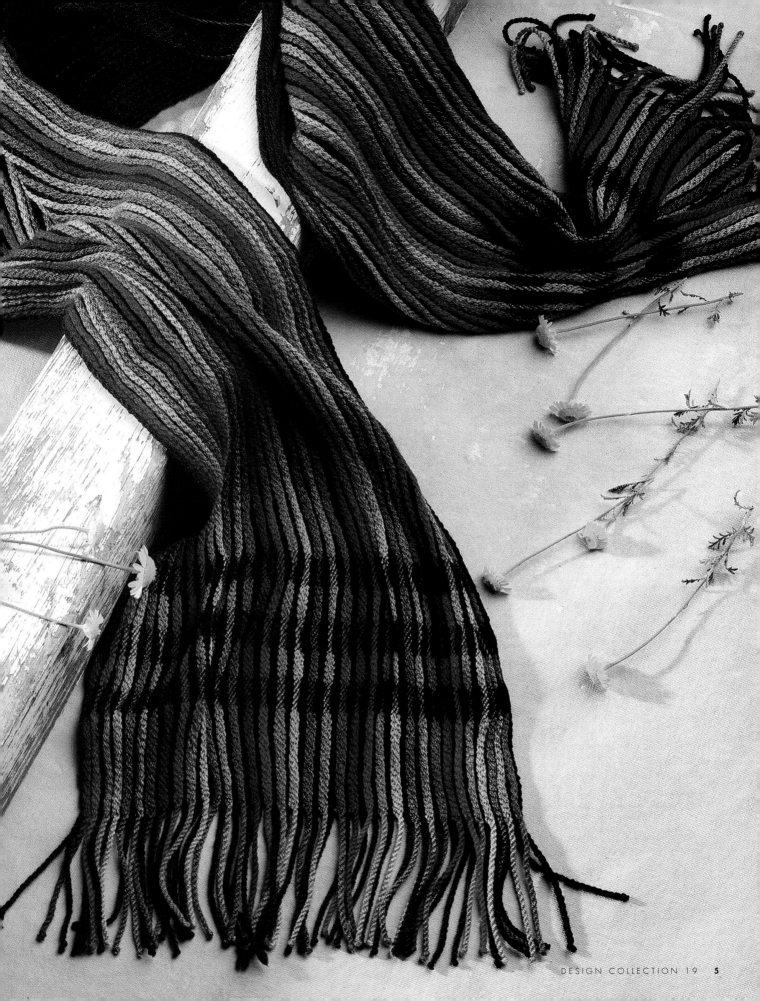

BLOOMING LEAF CHENILLE SCARF

JEAN KORUS

PROJECT AT-A-GLANCE

Weave structure
Shadow weave.

Equipment
4-shaft loom, 11" weaving width;
8-dent reed; 2 shuttles.

Yarns
Warp: Rayon chenille (1,450 yd/lb),
    burnt orange, 231 yd (2⅗ oz),
    and gold, 226 yd (2½ oz).
Weft: Rayon chenille (1,450 yd/lb),
    burnt orange and gold, 175 yd
    (2 oz) each.

Yarn sources
All of the yarns for this project were
provided by and are available from
Webs.

Warp order and length
164 ends (82 burnt orange ends alternating with 82 gold ends plus 2 burnt
orange ends for floating selvedges) 2¾
yd long (includes 26" for take-up,
loom waste, and fringe). Add 92" for
each additional scarf and fringe.

Warp and weft spacing
Warp: 16 epi (2/dent in an 8-dent
reed). Width in the reed: 10⅜".
Weft: 16 ppi.

Take-up and shrinkage
18% in width and 13% in length.
Amounts produce one scarf 8½" × 65"
not including fringe.

C henille is a luxurious yarn that makes a wonderfully rich, drapable fabric. Chenille especially loves shadow weave since the
bold patterning is created by color effects, not by long floats
that would allow the chenille to worm.

Project notes

In shadow weave, dark and light yarns alternate in both warp and weft. For the
pattern to show well, the two colors should contrast strongly with one another. If
you are considering colors other than burnt orange and gold, twist a strand of
each together and squint at them to see if they have enough contrast.

Wind two ends together on the warping board, one light and one dark, keep-
ing them separate with a finger. Check carefully for errors when threading. They
can be hard to spot and may not show up until the scarf has been wet-finished.
I place the draft on a magnetic board and move the magnet to show about four
threads at a time.

Weave a heading in plain weave with slick waste yarn such as nylon tricot
for about 8". Weave 1" with chenille (leaving a tail for hemstitching about three
times the width of the warp) "tromp as writ" (use the treadle number that corresponds to the shaft number in the threading and in the same color order). Hemstitch the first two rows enclosing groups of 4 ends and then weave for 72". Hemstitch and weave with 8–10" in scrap yarn.

Finishing

Remove the scarf from the loom and tie the ends in overhand knots to secure heading yarn. Your beautiful scarf feels like a board! Don't worry; finishing will make
it soft and supple. With a spray bottle filled with water, spray both sides thoroughly. Place the scarf in a plastic bag for several hours to wet evenly; machine
dry. Add a dryer sheet, if desired. Trim off the knots that secured the scrap heading yarn and remove the scrap yarn. Twist the fringe (see page 32) very tightly
using two hemstitched groups in each fringe. Steam the fringes, holding the iron
without touching them and using your hand to do the pressing. Instead of spraying, you can machine wash the scarf using a delicate cycle. I find spraying much
easier and haven't noticed any difference in the results.

1. Draft for scarf

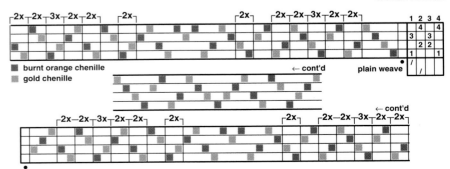

CHILD'S PLAY: A WINTER SCARF

LIZ GIPSON

PROJECT AT-A-GLANCE

Weave structure
4-shaft variation of twill blocks.

Equipment
4-shaft loom, 10" weaving width;
6-dent reed; 4 stick shuttles.

Yarns
Warp: worsted-weight wool and
cotton textured knitting yarn
(50% wool/50% cotton, 644 yd/lb,
Monterey), Grayed Teal and
Periwinkle, 35 yd (⅞ oz) each;
Grayed Blue and Brilliant Blush, 38
yd (1 oz) each.
Weft: worsted-weight wool and
cotton textured knitting yarn
(50% wool/50% cotton, 644 yd/lb,
Monterey), Grayed Teal, Grayed
Blue, Periwinkle, and Brilliant Blush,
32 yd (⅞ oz) each .

Yarn sources
Monterey knitting yarn is available
from Webs.

Warp order and length
56 ends (15 ends Brilliant Blush, 14
ends Grayed Teal, 14 ends Periwinkle,
and 15 ends Grayed Blue in the color
order in Figure 1) 2½ yd long (includes
2 ends for floating selvedges and 33"
for fringe, take-up, and loom waste).
Add 2 yd to warp length for each
additional scarf.

Warp and weft spacing
Warp: 6 epi (1/dent in a 6-dent
reed). Width in the reed: 9⅔".
Weft: about 8 ppi.

Take-up and shrinkage
28% in width and 13% in length.
Amounts produce one scarf 7" × 52"
plus fringe.

Children have very definite ideas about what they want to wear, so garments designed for them need to take their likes and dislikes into account. This brightly colored scarf is warm, soft, and durable enough to stand up to the rigors of winter fun. It is also proportioned to fit a small body.

The yarn used for the scarf is a textured, worsted-weight, 2-ply knitting yarn. One ply is a fine cotton and the other a lofty, loosely-spun wool. Knitting yarns are generally bulkier and softer than yarns designed for weaving, but the cotton ply makes this yarn strong enough to endure the stresses of the loom. Some experimenting was required to determine the sett and beat that would produce a stable fabric while preserving the yarn's lofty softness.

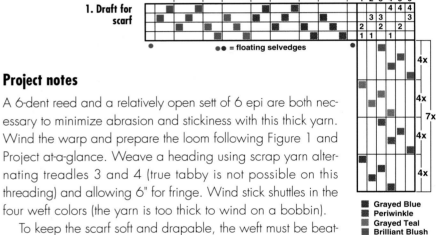

1. Draft for scarf

●● = floating selvedges

Grayed Blue
Periwinkle
Grayed Teal
Brilliant Blush

Project notes

A 6-dent reed and a relatively open sett of 6 epi are both necessary to minimize abrasion and stickiness with this thick yarn. Wind the warp and prepare the loom following Figure 1 and Project at-a-glance. Weave a heading using scrap yarn alternating treadles 3 and 4 (true tabby is not possible on this threading) and allowing 6" for fringe. Wind stick shuttles in the four weft colors (the yarn is too thick to wind on a bobbin).

To keep the scarf soft and drapable, the weft must be beaten in very gently. In fact, instead of "beating," gently bring the beater forward to place the yarn in the shed, maintaining a consistent density of 8 ppi. Begin with Brilliant Blush, and leaving a tail three times the width of the warp for hemstitching, weave the first 16 picks. End Brilliant Blush, thread a large tapestry needle with the tail, and hemstitch around two warp threads and two weft rows. Weave the rest of the scarf following the treadling and color order in Figure 1, ending each color at the end of each stripe (bring a small tail of weft back into the last shed of that color). At the end of the scarf, with a tail of the last weft (Grayed Blue) three times the width of the warp, hemstitch around pairs of warp threads as before.

Finishing

Remove the scarf from the loom allowing 6" for fringe at both ends. Wash the scarf gently by hand in warm water with a teaspoon of mild detergent. Rinse twice in water of the same temperature, and then roll in a towel to absorb excess water. Hang over a rod to dry. Trim the fringe evenly to 4" on each end. If necessary, use steam to remove any wrinkles with the iron on a wool setting.

THE MOBI-Q SHAWL
MARGO CARR

T his garment design is a hybrid of the Q-shawl and a Mobius strip. Unlike most shawls, the Mobi-Q needs little attention to keep it on the body.

Project notes

On eight shafts, all warp yarns except the Pazzaz bouclé are woven in plain weave. To take advantage of its shimmering color and textural interest, the Pazzaz weaves 2/2 twill on shafts 5–8. (Note that a 6-dent reed is essential to accommodate the irregularities of the Pazzaz.) The Mobi-Q can be woven in plain weave throughout on four shafts, but the Pazzaz will not show as much. Substitute another yarn if you wish. Beginning and ending with several repeats of scrap yarn, weave with Bordeaux following Figure 1 for 100". As you weave, the Chinchilla chenille may loosen; weight each end with an S-hook and a fishing weight.

Finishing

Remove the fabric from the loom and machine zigzag and then straight stitch each end. Remove scrap yarn and trim unwoven warp ends 1" from the stitched edge. Machine wash with a mild detergent, cold water, gentle cycle. Switch to the regular cycle to spin dry. Air dry over a line or rack, pulling gently to straighten the fabric. Do not press until after the garment is assembled.

Trim to stitching lines, turn raw edges ¼", and stitch. Lay fabric horizontally on a flat surface with stitched raw edges up and flip the left stitched raw edge over so that it faces down (see page 32). Move the left side of the fabric clockwise so that its selvedge overlaps the right stitched raw edge ½" and the left stitched edge extends ½". Topstitch along the overlapping selvedge of the left piece to connect the two pieces. To finish hems, turn under the left stitched edge, and topstitch. Topstitch along right edge. Press hems and seams using a velvet board or starched terry press cloth. The last task is to gently coax the chinchilla eyelashes out with the tip of a darning needle, and then your Mobi-Q is ready to wear!

1. Draft for Mobi-Q shawl

Threading repeats across: 6x, 3x, 10x, 2x, 3x, 8x, 3x, 9x (shafts 8–1; 2/2 twill on shafts 5–8).

2. Warp color order

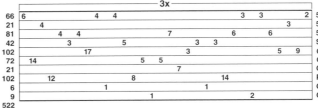

Ends	Color
66	5/2, Mute Blue
21	5/2, Dark Red
81	5/2, Dark Blue
42	Snowflake, Dark Turquoise
102	Gypsy Chenille, Dusky TurGreen
72	Gypsy Chenille, Bordeaux
21	Gypsy Chenille, Blue Velvet
102	Pazzaz, Maroon
6	Glacé, Fawn
9	Chinchilla Chenille, Turkish Navy
522	

A WINTER SCARF IN DORNIK TWILL

SCOTT NORRIS

PROJECT AT-A-GLANCE

Weave structure
Dornik twill.

Equipment
4-shaft loom, 12" weaving width;
10-dent reed; 2 shuttles.

Yarns
Warp: 14/2 wool/alpaca (3,920
yd/lb), Driftwood, 339 yd (1⅗ oz);
18/2 wool/silk (5,040 yd/lb),
Ebony, 339 yd (1⅛ oz).
Weft: 14/2 wool/alpaca (3,920
yd/lb), Coral Red, 243 yd (1 oz);
18/2 wool/silk (5,040 yd/lb),
Ebony, 243 yd (⅘ oz).

Yarn sources
JaggerSpun wool/alpaca and
wool/silk are from Webs and are
available from most weaving retailers.

Warp order and length
226 ends alternating Driftwood
wool/alpaca and Ebony wool/silk
3 yd long; includes 2 ends for floating
selvedges (allows 38" for fringe, take-
up, and loom waste). Add 90" for
each additional scarf.

Warp and weft spacing
Warp: 20 epi (2/dent in a 10-dent
reed). Width in the reed: 11⅓".
Weft: 20 ppi.

Take-up and shrinkage
12% in width and 12% in length.
Amounts produce one scarf 10" × 64"
plus fringe.

A combination of a classic dornik threading, an "on opposites" treadling, and a blend of black, coral, and gray-brown yarns produces a darkly colorful fabric with a moody, irregular pattern that resembles a chain of flowers. Mixing black in both warp and weft brings the design into sharp focus.

Project notes

A 3-yd warp weaves one 64" scarf. Add 90" warp length for each additional scarf. Wind the warp and thread the loom following Figure 1 and Project at-a-glance. Allowing about 9" at the beginning and end for fringe, weave a heading with scrap yarn. Then, using two shuttles, weave following the treadling in Figure 1 for 70". End with scrap yarn to secure edges until the fringe is worked.

When you are weaving with two shuttles, it is a good idea to experiment with shuttle order and placement to determine which way produces the smoothest selvedges. Once you have found the best method, use it consistently and avoid tangled shuttles and selvedge irregularities by always placing the same shuttle in the same place while you throw the other. A very light touch is all that is required to beat this fabric to square.

Finishing

Remove the fabric from the loom and prepare a twisted fringe (see page 32). For this scarf, tightly twist two adjacent groups of 5 ends each separately to the right; then join the two groups and twist them together tightly to the left and secure the combined strand with an overhand knot. Remove the scrap yarn as you work the fringe and trim the ends close to the knots.

Wash the scarf by hand, immersing it in cold water with a few drops of mild detergent. Agitate it gently for a moment, and then allow the scarf to soak for three minutes undisturbed before rinsing it in cold water until the water runs clear. Handle the fabric carefully without scrubbing, pulling, or wringing.

Remove excess water from the scarf by rolling it in a towel; repeat with a second towel. Hang the scarf over a rod padded with a towel until completely dry. If faint wrinkles remain after the scarf is fully dry, pad an ironing board with a towel, lay the scarf on the ironing board and cover it with another towel or a sheet. Lightly press with a warm, not hot, iron.

1. Draft for scarf

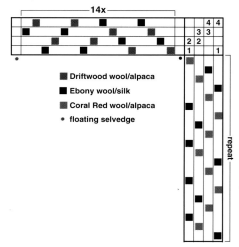

■ Driftwood wool/alpaca
■ Ebony wool/silk
■ Coral Red wool/alpaca
• floating selvedge

DOUBLEWEAVE FOR A WOOL RUANA

BETSY BLUMENTHAL

PROJECT AT-A-GLANCE

Weave structure
Two layers of plain weave.

Equipment
4-shaft loom, 21" weaving width;
8-dent reed; 2 shuttles.

Yarns
Warp: 2-ply wool (900 yd/lb), Russet,
   581 yd (10⅓ oz); Iris, 196 yd
   (3½ oz); Aubergine and Teal Blue,
   168 yd (3 oz) each; Cobalt, 42 yd
   (¾ oz).
Weft: 2-ply wool (1,800 yd/lb),
   Midnight Blue, 605 yd (5⅜ oz);
   Plum, 195 yd (1¾ oz).

Yarn sources
Harrisville Highland wool (900 yd/lb)
and Shetland wool (1,800 yd/lb) are
available from most weaving retailers.

Warp order and length
330 ends 3½ yd long (includes 44"
for take-up, loom waste, and fringe).

Warp and weft spacing
Warp: 16 epi (8 epi/layer, 2/dent
in an 8-dent reed, except sley last 4
ends on the right 1/dent). Width in
the reed: 20⅞". Weft: 16 ppi
(8 ppi/layer).

Take-up and shrinkage
13% in width and 15% in length.
Amounts produce one ruana 36" ×
72" unfolded, not including fringe.

A ruana is a poncho that is open down the front and closed in the back. It is often worn like a shawl with one of the front panels wrapped over the opposite shoulder. Its unique construction makes the ruana ideal to weave as two layers.

Project notes

The weaving is done using the doubleweave draft in Figure 1. The first half of the cloth (the back of the ruana) is woven with one shuttle in two layers that are connected at one side. When the cloth is removed from the loom, this half of the fabric will unfold to twice the width of the warp. The second half of the fabric (the front of the ruana) is woven with two shuttles to form two unconnected layers that become the front pieces.

Allow 8–10" for fringe, weave a 1–2" heading in scrap yarn, and then weave the ruana following Figures 1 and 3. Be sure to clear the shed carefully before each pick to avoid catching threads between layers. Some weavers mount a mirror on the side of the loom so they can see any warp threads that are out of place in the shed. End with 1–2" scrap yarn.

1. Draft for ruana

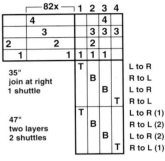

T = top layer
B = bottom layer
L = left
R = right
(1) = shuttle 1
(2) = shuttle 2

2. Warp color order

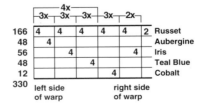

left side   right side
of warp   of warp

The right side of the warp is the center of the ruana. When the ruana is opened, there will be one extra Iris and one extra Russet warp thread in the center.

3. Weft color order

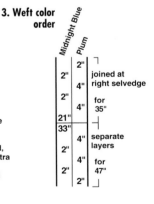

Finishing

Cut the fabric from the loom and correct weaving errors (if any warp ends have caught weft threads in the wrong layer, pull them out for a few inches and needle weave them into the proper layer). Remove waste yarn and make a twisted fringe (see page 32) using 4 ends (2/2) in each fringe for a barber-pole effect. The two center twists will have an extra Russet end in their bundles.

Full the wool either by washing firmly by hand in warm water or by agitating 2–3 minutes in an automatic washer. Rinse by filling and draining two times with minimum agitation; then drain and spin briefly on a gentle setting. Dry flat.

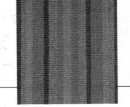

SOFT AND SILKY WARP-FACED SCARF

SUZANNE DeATLEY

PROJECT AT-A-GLANCE

Weave structure
Warp-faced plain weave.

Equipment
4-shaft loom, 9" weaving width;
10-dent reed; 1 shuttle.

Yarns
Warp: 18/2 wool/silk (5,040 yd/lb),
   Charcoal, 187 yd (⅗ oz); Violet,
   214 yd (⁷⁄₁₀ oz); Cassis, 174 yd (⅗
   oz); Copper, 294 yd (1 oz).
Weft: 18/2 wool/silk (5,040 yd/lb),
   Charcoal, 62 yd (⅕ oz).

Yarn sources
18/2 wool/silk (Zephyr by Jagger-
Spun) is available from most weaving
retailers.

Warp order and length
325 ends 2⅔ yd long, following the
warp color order in Figure 1 (allows
40" for fringe, take-up, and loom
waste).

Warp and weft spacing
Warp: 40 epi (4/dent in a 10-dent
reed). Width in the reed: 8⅛".
Weft: 5 ppi.

Take-up and shrinkage
2% in width and 12% in length (most
of this is take-up since the fabric is
warp-faced). Amounts produce one
scarf 8" × 49½" plus fringe.

Have you ever had the experience of winding a glorious striped warp only to find the colors dulled by the interlacing weft? To show off the rich sheen and lovely colors of a luxurious wool/silk yarn in my stash, the warp in this scarf is sett closely so that the weft barely shows. We think of warp-faced plain weave as creating a sturdy, durable fabric used mainly for rugs and mats. To achieve the right hand for a scarf, I experimented with different warp and weft setts and discovered that if the weft is too dense, the fabric becomes stiff and dull. For these yarns, a warp sett of 40 epi and a very open weft sett of 5 ppi produce a light and lustrous fabric with an exquisite drape.

Project notes

Wind the warp and thread the loom for plain weave following Project at-a-glance and the warp color order in Figure 1. Allow 10" for fringe and weave 52" in plain weave at a consistent 5 ppi. Measure as you go! The weft must be beaten very gently to achieve such an open sett. In fact, "beat" is probably a misnomer—place the weft straight in the shed (you do not need to allow extra weft to prevent draw-in since in warp-faced weaves most of the take-up is in the warp), and bring the beater forward. A slightly softer warp tension than usual may also be helpful to avoid beating the weft too densely.

The close sett of 40 epi makes this warp a bit sticky. To facilitate forming clear sheds, place the weft, move the beater to the fell, and change treadles to form the next shed before moving the beater back toward the shafts. As you move it back, the beater will help separate the sticky yarns for the new shed.

1. Warp color order						
70	20	15		15	20	Charcoal
80	15	25		25	15	Violet
65		20	25		20	Cassis
110		35	20	20	35	Copper
325						

Finishing

Remove the scarf from the loom allowing 10" for fringe. Prepare a twisted fringe (see page 32). Choose the number of threads for each fringe that makes a pleasing arrangement. (I kept the fringe colors solid for most of the stripes and mixed the colors only where necessary to maintain consistent fringe thickness.) Measuring 6" from the fabric edge, tie an overhand knot to secure each fringe. Trim the fringe evenly below the knots.

This is a delicate fabric, so handle it gently during finishing. Wash the scarf by hand with a drop of shampoo, rinse it with a conditioning rinse, and then roll it in a large absorbent towel to blot excess water before hanging to dry. When it is dry, steam press it lightly using a press cloth to bring up the sheen.

SILK HUCK LACE SHAWLS FOR SPRING

RUTH MORRISON

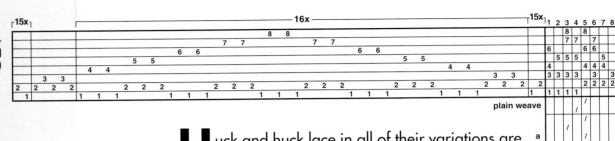

1. Draft for 8-shaft shawl (right, p. 19)

plain weave

H uck and huck lace in all of their variations are beautiful in wool, cotton, and linen—but in silk they become sumptuous miracles!

2. Draft for 4-shaft shawl (left, p. 19)

plain weave

PROJECT AT-A-GLANCE

Weave structure
Huck and huck lace.

Equipment
4-shaft or 8-shaft loom, 25" weaving width; 12-dent reed; 1 shuttle.

Yarns
Warp: 30/2 silk (7,500 yd/lb), natural, 2,595 yd (5⅗ oz).
Weft: 30/2 silk (7,500 yd/lb), natural, 1,720 yd (3⅔ oz).

Yarn sources
30/2 silk is available in 1,540 yd (3½ oz) skeins from the Yarn Barn. Three skeins are needed for one shawl.

Notions and other materials
750 size 11° seed beads in a color similar to the silk, beading needle, strong fine thread. (Beads, needles, and beading thread are available from retail bead and craft stores.)

Warp order and length
865 ends 3 yd long (allows 36" for fringe, take-up, and loom waste).

Warp and weft spacing
Warp: 36 epi (3/dent in a 12-dent reed). Width in the reed: 24¹⁄₁₆".
Weft: 32 ppi.

Take-up and shrinkage
6% in width and 8% in length. Amounts produce one shawl 22½" × 68½" plus 9" fringe.

Project notes

It is very important to maintain a consistent beat with lace weaves. As you weave, watch the plain-weave selvedge sections to see that they look even. Beat lightly in the 4-shaft lace areas—the many floats want to pack in! Allow 12" for fringe at each end. Hemstitch, encircling 6 ends and 2 weft rows in each group.

Finishing

Remove the fabric from the loom and twist the fringe (see page 2), using two hemstitched groups for each fringe. Hand wash in hot water with mild liquid detergent. Rinse several times in water of the same temperature; add vinegar to the second rinse and fabric softener to the last rinse. Squeeze out water, roll shawl in a towel to remove excess water, and hang to dry out of direct sunlight. Steam press on a wool setting using a press cloth.

Beading in the fringe can add weight, movement, and a subtle sparkle to the shawl. With a beading needle, anchor the beading thread into the edge of the shawl. Bring the needle out between the two hemstitches of the first twisted fringe, and stitch one bead. Then run the needle to the center between the first two fringes, thread 4 beads on the needle, slide the beads up the thread to the fell of the cloth, and take the needle back through the first 3 beads. Needle weave through the edge of the shawl to the next space at the center of the next fringe and place another single bead. Bring the needle out between the next two fringes, make a 4-bead fringe, and repeat across the width of the shawl at each end.

Weave 1" plain weave.
Weave a, b, c, d, e, f, e, d, c, b. Repeat for 70". Balance at end with a. Weave 1" plain weave.

Use two treadles where indicated.

Weave 1" plain weave.
Weave from * to * 9x:
*[a, b] 2x
[c, d] 3x
c
[b, a] 2x
[d, c] 3x
d*
Weave (to balance):
[a, b] 2x.
Weave 1" plain weave.

SPRING FLOWERS SHAWL

HELEN BOBISUD

PROJECT AT-A-GLANCE

Weave structure
Advancing twill.

Equipment
8-shaft loom, 26" weaving width; 12-dent reed; 2 shuttles, 7 bobbins.

Yarns
Warp: 18/2 wool/silk (5,040 yd/lb), Curry, 60 yd (⅕ oz); Plum, 588 yd (1⅞ oz); Elderberry, Lilac, Teal, Juniper, and Peacock, 294 yd (1⁵⁄₁₆ oz) each.

Weft: 18/2 wool/silk (5,040 yd/lb), Curry, 38 yd (⅛ oz); Plum, 344 yd (1⅛ oz); Elderberry, Lilac, Teal, Juniper, and Peacock, 271 yd (⅞ oz) each.

The above amounts of wool/silk can be purchased as eight 600-yd minicones: Plum, 2 minicones; Curry, Elderberry, Lilac, Teal, Juniper, and Peacock, 1 minicone each.

Yarn sources
18/2 wool/silk (Zephyr by Jagger-Spun) is available in 600-yd minicones from Halcyon Yarns and in larger cones from most suppliers.

Warp order and length
605 ends (includes 1 end Curry on each side for floating selvedges) 3½ yd long (allows 28" for take-up, fringe, and loom waste).

Warp and weft spacing
Warp: 24 epi (2/dent in a 12-dent reed). Width in the reed: 25¼". Weft: 22 ppi.

Take-up and shrinkage
11% in width and 9% in length. Amounts produce one shawl 22½" × 89" not including fringe.

A warm but light shawl is the perfect wrap for cool spring nights. This shawl uses a wool/silk yarn in cool hues with a subtle accent of warm gold. Using the same colors in warp and weft causes the design to seem to appear and disappear.

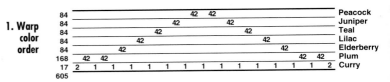

1. Warp color order

Project notes

Allow 12" of warp (include the yarn used to tie on to the apron rod) for fringe. Begin and end with 3 picks plain weave using Plum and hemstitch over these picks in groups of 5 ends. Following weft color order, weave "tromp as writ" (step on the treadle that corresponds to each shaft number in Figure 3). Avoid drawing in; use a temple, if available.

Finishing

Remove the fabric from the loom, remove scrap yarn, and loosely tie fringe ends in large bunches with overhand knots. Hand wash in barely warm water with a very small amount of mild detergent; swish gently. Dye will come out in the water. Drain and gently squeeze out excess water. Rinse two or three times. After the last rinse, roll shawl in a towel to absorb water. Hang over a padded rod or lay flat to dry.

While the shawl is still slightly damp, untie knots in fringe and steam press shawl and fringe with the iron on a wool setting. Make a twisted fringe (see page 32) using two hemstitched warp groups in each fringe. To bring out the luster of the yarn, dampen the fabric and steam press firmly (wool setting) on both sides excluding the fringe.

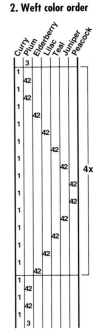

2. Weft color order

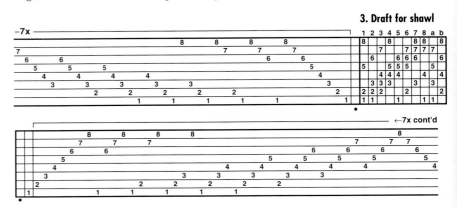

3. Draft for shawl

Please don't sit on my arms!

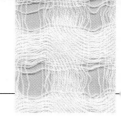

A TWILL SCARF THAT'S LIGHT AS AIR

MARCELLA LAUGHLIN AND MARY FROST

PROJECT AT-A-GLANCE

Weave structure
2/2 twill with grouped and spaced warp and weft threads.

Equipment
4-shaft loom, 10" weaving width; 10-dent reed; 1 shuttle; 1 cardboard strip 1" × 10–11" to use for weft spacer.

Yarns
Warp: 18/2 merino wool (5,040 yd/lb), natural white, 600 yd (2 oz).
Weft: 18/2 merino wool (5,040 yd/lb), natural white, 370 yd (1⅜ oz).

Yarn sources
18/2 merino wool by JaggerSpun is available from most weaving retailers.

Warp order and length
200 ends 3 yd long (includes 39" for fringe, take-up, and loom waste). Allow 2⅛ yd warp length for each additional scarf and fringe.

Warp and weft spacing
Warp: 1" at 40 epi alternates with 1" of empty dents (sley 40 ends 4/dent in a 10-dent reed; leave 10 empty dents following Figure 1). Width in the reed: 9". Weft: 1" at 40 ppi alternates with 1" unwoven warp.

Take-up and shrinkage
8% in width and 8% in length. Amounts produce one scarf 8¼" × 63½" plus fringe.

Who would think that wool woven in a sturdy 2/2 twill could make a delicate, lacy, and almost weightless scarf? It's not only possible, but easy—just leave some air between the threads! In this scarf, squares of 2/2 twill alternate with unwoven spaces. The threads nearest the unwoven areas slip, forming a soft, lacy frame of yarn around the spaces. To minimize slipping, the sett in the woven areas is somewhat close, and wool is the fiber of choice.

Project notes

The spaces in the warp are a result of the denting. Groups of 40 ends sleyed 4/dent alternate with ten empty dents. Thread and sley following Figure 1. Allow 9" for fringe and weave a few picks of scrap yarn. Beating firmly, weave the first 40 picks with merino weft. Open the shed for the spacer and insert the cardboard strip. Carry the weft over the spacer and into the first shed of the next section of twill, tensioning the weft so that it is like the warp. Weave 40 picks. Remove the cardboard from the first space and insert it into the shed for the spacer. Continue for 65" and end with a few picks of scrap yarn.

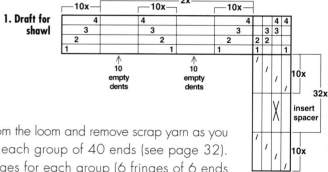

1. Draft for shawl

Finishing

Remove the fabric from the loom and remove scrap yarn as you twist the fringes for each group of 40 ends (see page 32). Work 7 twisted fringes for each group (6 fringes of 6 ends arranged 3/3 and one fringe of 4 arranged 2/2). For a sculpted effect, the lengths of the fringes can be varied by tying the overhand knot that secures the fringe at a different place (in this scarf, the fringe is shorter on the outer stripes (2–3" on one side, 5–6" on the other) and becomes longer toward the center (7"). Trim each fringe below the knot.

Wet finishing must be done very carefully—the woven yarns tend to migrate into the unwoven areas. Wash by hand in warm (not hot) water with a little Orvus paste or mild dishwashing detergent. Allow to soak for 5 minutes; then gently squeeze and work the scarf, agitating it as little as possible. Remove the scarf from the soapy water and rinse twice in clear water of the same temperature, adding a splash of vinegar to the first rinse if desired.

Gently squeeze out excess water, roll in a towel, and lay flat to dry. Press with a steam iron using a press cloth.

NIGHT WINDOWS SCARF FOR FOUR OR EIGHT SHAFTS

BARBARA WEISSMAN

PROJECT AT-A-GLANCE

Weave structure
Plain weave on four shafts, a combination of twill and plain weave on eight shafts.

Equipment
4-shaft or 8-shaft loom, 10–13" weaving width; 8-dent reed; 2 shuttles.

Yarns
Warp: 5/2 pearl cotton (2,100 yd/lb), black, 480 yd (3⅔ oz); variegated rayon chenille (1,300 yd/lb), Kenya #039, 108 yd (1⅓ oz).
Weft: 100% viscose (2,325 yd/lb), black, 250 yd (1¾ oz); variegated rayon chenille (1,300 yd/lb), Kenya #039, 87 yd (1⅛ oz).

Yarn sources
Chenille Tapestry (variegated rayon chenille) and Marbella viscose are available from Silk City Fibers, 5/2 pearl cotton from most suppliers.

Warp order and length
196 ends (160 pearl cotton, 36 chenille) 3 yd long (includes 36" for take-up, loom waste, and fringe): [16 black, 4 chenille] 9x; 16 black. Add 96" for each additional scarf and fringe.

Warp and weft spacing
Warp for 4-shaft scarf: 16 epi (2/dent in an 8-dent reed). Width in the reed: 12¼" (for a narrower scarf, eliminate one or two repeats). Warp for 8-shaft scarf: 21 epi for black pearl cotton, 16 epi for chenille. (In an 8-dent reed, sley each block of 16 ends pearl cotton 3-2-3-3-2-3, and each 4-end block of chenille 2/dent). Width in the reed: 9⅞". Weft: 13 ppi.

Take-up and shrinkage
20% in width and 17% in length. Amounts produce one scarf 9⅞" × 59½" plus fringe on four shafts, 7⅞" × 59½" plus fringe on eight.

I designed this scarf as a project for our guild's weave structure study group. It combines several simple design ideas. Black intensifies the colors near it, so I used it as a background to set off the jewel-like colors of a shimmering variegated rayon chenille. Pearl cotton as the background warp and rayon as the background weft add depth to the black hue and a luxurious hand to the scarf.

Weave the scarf on four shafts in plain weave or in a combination of twill and plain weave on eight. To make the 4-shaft scarf the same width as the 8-shaft scarf, remove two of the repeats in the warp color order (see Project at-a-glance and replace 9x with 7x) for a finished width of about 8".

Project notes
Wind the warp and thread the loom as in Project at-a-glance and Figure 1. Note that on eight shafts the black pearl cotton is sleyed 3-2-3-3-2-3 for each 16-thread section, while the 4 ends of chenille are sleyed 2/dent. All of the warp threads in the 4-shaft scarf are sleyed 2/dent.

Begin by weaving a heading allowing 8–10" for fringe, and then weave 3" of chenille in plain weave to add weight and a border to the scarf. Weave 12 picks black rayon and 3 picks chenille either in plain weave or following Figure 1 for 66". End with the second border of 3" plain weave in chenille.

A weft sett of 13 ppi produces slightly rectangular windows. The number of black picks can be varied for different effects. To avoid loops of chenille at the selvedges, catch the chenille weft with the black rayon along the edges of the scarf as you weave.

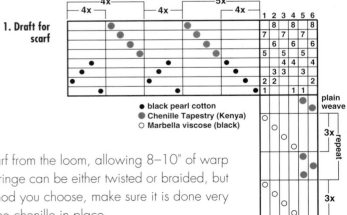

1. Draft for scarf

● black pearl cotton
● Chenille Tapestry (Kenya)
○ Marbella viscose (black)

Finishing
Remove the scarf from the loom, allowing 8–10" of warp for fringe. The fringe can be either twisted or braided, but whichever method you choose, make sure it is done very tightly to hold the chenille in place.

After twisting or braiding and knotting the fringe, wash the scarf by hand in warm water with a mild detergent. Roll it tightly in a towel to blot up excess water, and then dry it in the dryer on a hot setting. As soon as it is dry, steam press the scarf and trim the "fuzzies" from the ends of the fringe.

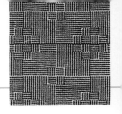

LAVENDER SHADOWS SCARVES

GUDRUN POLAK

PROJECT AT-A-GLANCE

Weave structure
Shadow weave.

Equipment
8-shaft loom, 9" weaving width; 12-dent reed; 2 shuttles; weights for floating selvedges (2–3" S-hooks work well).

Yarns
Warp: 20/2 spun Bombyx silk (5,000 yd/lb), deep purple JY23, 288 yd (1 oz); lavender, JY50, 288 yd (1 oz). 8/2 reeled Bombyx silk (2,800 yd/lb), 4 yd (1/16 oz) each red orange #9513 and orange JY36 for accent color floating selvedges.
Weft: 20/2 spun Bombyx silk (5,000 yd/lb), 225 yd (¾ oz) each black JY57 (or deep purple JY23) and lavender JY50.

Yarn sources
20/2 spun silk and 8/2 reeled silk are available from Treenway Silks.

Warp order and length
192 ends alternating 1 end deep purple and 1 end lavender 3 yd long (includes 32" for fringe, take-up, and loom waste). Add 1 end orange and 1 end red-orange 4 yd long for floating selvedges after threading. Allow 96" warp length for each additional scarf and fringe.

Warp and weft spacing
Warp: 24 epi (2/dent in a 12-dent reed). Width in the reed: 8½". Weft: 25 ppi.

Take-up and shrinkage
13% in width and 13% in length. Amounts produce one scarf 7" × 66½".

Resources
Fry, Laura. "All about Wet Finishing," HANDWOVEN, January/February 2001, pp. 28–31.

These silk scarves are woven in classic shadow weave using a versatile threading that can produce many different designs. The scarves use a border design of nested squares and a design I call "bouncing ball" for the center field. Two contrasting colors—deep purple and lavender—alternate in both warp and weft. For an element of surprise, the floating selvedges are heavier threads of orange and red-orange, and to give more definition to the design, black replaces purple in the weft of the scarf on the left.

Project notes

Add a red-orange silk end to one side of the warp and an orange silk end to the other for floating selvedges; weight. Allow 8" for fringe and weave a plain-weave heading with scrap yarn alternating treadles 3 and 4. With a shuttle of black (or purple) and one of lavender, weave two repeats with treadling a for the nested squares border. Although you can arrange a tie-up for 10 treadles, the treadling is easier to follow if you use eight and change the tie-up of treadles 5–6 to weave the bouncing ball design (weave treadling b 24x). Then retie treadles 5–6 and weave with treadling a 2x for the second border. Weave a few picks of scrap yarn and remove the scarf from the loom allowing 8" for fringe.

Finishing

For fringe, tie overhand knots in groups of 8 ends to correspond with the design blocks. Wash the scarf by hand in hot water with a drop of liquid dishwashing detergent. Rinse in water of the same temperature. Roll in a towel to remove excess water. While it is still quite damp, give the scarf a hard press until dry (press down firmly with the iron rather than sliding it back and forth).

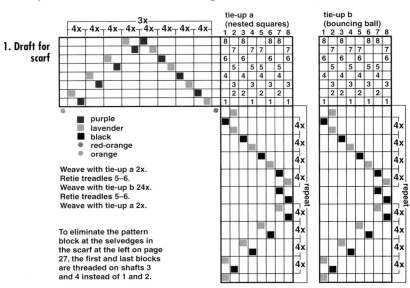

1. Draft for scarf

tie-up a (nested squares)

tie-up b (bouncing ball)

■ purple
▨ lavender
■ black
● red-orange
● orange

Weave with tie-up a 2x.
Retie treadles 5–6.
Weave with tie-up b 24x.
Retie treadles 5–6.
Weave with tie-up a 2x.

To eliminate the pattern block at the selvedges in the scarf at the left on page 27, the first and last blocks are threaded on shafts 3 and 4 instead of 1 and 2.

PEACOCK SHAWL IN SHINY TENCEL
HORACE LETHBRIDGE

PROJECT AT-A-GLANCE

Weave structure
Straight, point, and broken twill and plain weave.

Equipment
8-shaft loom, 14" weaving width; 12-dent reed; 1 shuttle; rotary cutter and ruler (optional).

Yarns
Warp: 10/2 Tencel (4,200 yd/lb), Moroccan Blue, 1,096 yd (4³/₁₆ oz).
Weft: 10/2 Tencel (4,200 yd/lb), Emerald, 891 yd (3²/₅ oz).

Yarn sources
10/2 Tencel is available from Textura Trading Company.

Warp order and length
329 ends 3⅓ yd long (includes 31" for fringe, take-up, and loom waste). Add 3 yd to warp length for each additional shawl. (Consider weaving several shawls, each with a different weft color.)

Warp and weft spacing
Warp: 24 epi (2/dent in a 12-dent reed). Width in the reed: 13¾". Weft: 24 ppi.

Take-up and shrinkage
10% in width and 10% in length. Amounts produce one shawl 12½" × 80½" plus fringe.

This winsome fabric, woven in two closely related colors of 10/2 Tencel, shares both its colors and a touch of iridescence with peacock feathers. The pattern is the result of designing fancy twill threadings using straight and point twill progressions and surrounding the twill designs with plain weave.

1. Draft for shawl

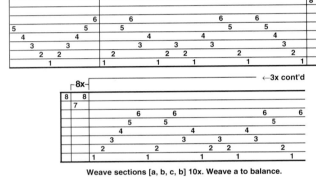

Weave sections [a, b, c, b] 10x. Weave a to balance.

Project notes

The twill tie-up used for the shawl produces 3-thread floats in a background of plain weave. The result is an intricate pattern that exploits the contrast between the sheen of the Tencel floats and the matte plainweave.

Project dimensions are appropriate for a dressy shawl but also suitable for a large scarf. For a larger shawl add one threading repeat (each repeat is 4⅓" wide) or for a narrower scarf eliminate one repeat.

Allowing 4" for fringe, leave a tail of weft three times the width of the warp and weave the first plain-weave section (a). Then use the weft tail to hemstitch over the first two weft rows around groups of 4 ends. Weave the rest of the shawl following Figure 1 and hemstitch.

Finishing

Remove the shawl from the loom and trim the fringe at each end to 3" using a ruler and rotary cutter. Wash by hand in warm water with a mild liquid detergent. Rinse thoroughly in cool water. Roll in a towel to blot up excess water and then hang to dry, smoothing out any creases. At this point the fabric will look stiff and dull. Steam press on both sides to bring out the luster of the Tencel, the iridescence produced by the colors, and the delicacy of the design.

A NEW MILLENNIUM QUECHQUEMITL

SARA LAMB

PROJECT AT-A-GLANCE

Weave structure
Plain weave.

Equipment
2-shaft or 4-shaft loom, 28" weaving width; 10-dent reed; 1 shuttle.

Yarns
Warp: 3-ply wool fingering yarn (2,800 yd/lb, 310 yd/50 gm skein), 2,800 yd total: #235 Beet Red, 930 yd (5⅓ oz); #48 Scarlet, 750 yd (4⅓ oz); #17 French Clay, 500 yd (2⅞ oz); #308 Sunburst Gold, 400 yd (2⅓ oz); #62 Amethyst, 100 yd (⅔ oz); #305 Impasse Yellow, 70 yd (⅖ oz); and #11 Emerald Fantasy, 50 yd (⅓ oz).
Weft: 3-ply wool fingering yarn, #200 Bordeaux, 1,881 yd (10¾ oz).

Yarn sources
NatureSpun 100% wool 3-ply fingering yarn by Brown Sheep Company is available from Shuttles, Spindles & Skeins.

Notions and other materials
Sewing thread to match fabric.

Warp order and length
Warp: 560 total ends 5 yd long (allows 24" take-up and loom waste). Main warp: 516 ends following the color order in Figure 1. Three accent warps: 14 ends Impasse Yellow, 20 ends Amethyst, 10 ends Emerald Fantasy.

Warp and weft spacing
Main and accent warps: 20 epi (2/dent in a 10-dent reed). Width in the reed: 28". Weft: 14 ppi.

Take-up and shrinkage
5% in width and 8% in length. Amounts produce a piece of yardage 26½" × 4 yd, enough for one quechquemitl and cowl neckline insert.

The quechquemitl is an elegantly simple garment consisting of two rectangles sewn end-to-side in the back and front. This version adds two design ideas to the traditional shape making a garment that is contemporary and convenient.

Project notes
Wind the main warp and the three accent warps following Figure 1. Sley each accent warp 2/dent randomly across the warp width (28"). Sley the main warp 2/dent in all dents that do not have accent threads. Thread for plain weave, beam, and weave with Bordeaux weft for the length of the warp (about 4⅓ yd).

Finishing
Remove the fabric from the loom. Machine zigzag ends. Fill washing machine with hot water; soak fabric for one hour. Agitate briefly, guarding against over-fulling. Spin out water, steam press fabric on a wool setting, and lay flat to dry.

When the rectangles of a quechquemitl are short enough to create a small neckline, the shoulders prevent the neckline from lying flat. If the rectangles are longer, the garment molds nicely over the shoulders but the neck opening is too large. The solution in this design is to make the rectangles long and sew a cowl-neck insert in the large V-neck opening.

Cut two rectangles 50" long, baste together (see Figure 2) to check fit, and then sew seams by machine. Cut two pieces for the neckline insert (see Figure 3). Adjust width of neck opening by practicing with a muslin. Right sides together, stitch side seams. Turn right side out, turn bottom edge under ½", press, and topstitch to V-neck opening. To reduce hem bulk, mark a straight horizontal line 25" up from the points in the front and back; cut. Machine zigzag raw edge, turn under once and topstitch ¼" from the edge. Topstitch a second row closer to the fold. Press.

1. Warp color order

Main warp

	26x	14x	86x		
186			1	100	Beet Red
150		1	50	1	Scarlet
100	1	60	1		French Clay
80	54	1			Sunburst Gold
516					

Three accent warps
20 ends Amethyst
14 ends Impasse Yellow
10 ends Emerald Fantasy

2. Quechquemitl construction

Sew two seams (indicated by stitching lines).

3. Pattern for neckline insert

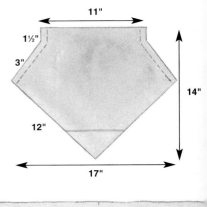

11"

1½"

3"

12"

14"

17"

READING DRAFTS

Read the threading draft from right to left. Floating selvedges are noted by bullets (a floating selvedge is a warp thread on each side of the warp that is sleyed but not threaded). Floating selvedges can be beamed with the warp or suspended from the back of the loom. In either case, they should each be weighted; a 3" S-hook works well. Enter the shuttle in the shed *over* the floating selvedge and exit the shuttle *under* it.)

Brackets in the draft indicate repeated sections. For more than one level of brackets, repeat first the sections closest to the draft.

Numbers in the tie-up indicate the shafts that are raised. Read the treadling sequence from top to bottom starting with the first mark below the tie-up.

Colors of individual ends and picks are sometimes indicated by letters (or colors) in the threading and treadling drafts with a key (O = orange, for example). In other cases a color order chart is given in which each row or column represents a color. Read a warp color order chart from right to left just as you read a threading draft, but note that the rows indicate colors instead of shafts. Read a weft color order chart the same way you read a treadling draft, from top to bottom, except each column is a color, not a treadle.

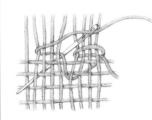

Draft

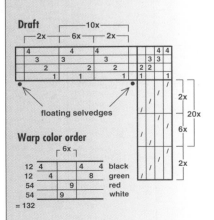

floating selvedges

Warp color order

12	4		4		4	black
12	4				8	green
54				9		red
54		9				white
= 132						

WEAVING AND FINISHING

Weaving tips

Project directions give the number of inches allowed for take-up and loom waste (fringe is taken from loom waste). Note that for large floor looms, loom waste can be as much as 40" and adjust warp length accordingly.

Some of the warp color orders are complicated and require many yarns. It is always possible to make yarn substitutions. For best results, use the same type of fiber (cotton, wool, silk, etc.) of about the same thickness.

The projects by Helen Bobisud and Jean Korus give the treadling instructions as "tromp as writ." For these, use the threading draft as the treadling draft. Each treadle is numbered. If the first thread in the threading draft is on shaft 4, you step on treadle 4 and weave a pick. If the next thread is on shaft 2, you step on treadle 2, and continue, following the numbers in the threading.

Scarves and shawls can be many different sizes. One rule of thumb for the length of a scarf is your own height. Almost all of the pieces in this collection would be just as successful at different sizes. Add to the width and length of a scarf to make a shawl and vice versa. Most of the pieces are finished with hemstitching or a twisted fringe.

Twisted fringe

Divide the number of strands for each fringe into two groups. Holding a group in each hand, twist each group clockwise until it kinks. Bring both of the groups together in one hand and allow them to twist around each other counterclockwise (or twist them in that direction). Secure the end with an overhand knot.

Simple hemstitching

Thread a tail of weft three times warp width into a tapestry needle. Take the needle under the group of ends above the fell and bring it up and back to the starting point, encircling the group. Pass the needle under the same group of ends, bringing it out through the weaving two (or more) weft threads below the fell. Repeat for each group of ends across the fell. Needle weave the tail into the selvedge and trim.

Assembling the Mobi-Q (from pages 10–11)

Begin with both stitched raw edges up. Turn over the left edge (twisting the fabric). Bring the left edge (a) up clockwise to overlap the right stitched raw edge (extending about ½"). Topstitch along selvedge of the left piece to join the two pieces (b). Fold the left edge (a) over the right top selvedge and top stitch along both folds. Topstitch along fold of right edge (under the selvedge at b).

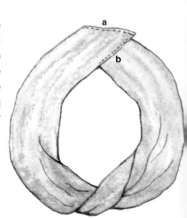